MW01600804

Debt to Wealth
Mastering Financial Leverage

Disclaimer

The information contained in this book, "Debt to Wealth: Mastering Financial Leverage," is provided for informational purposes only. The author and publisher are not financial advisors, and the content of this book is not intended to be a substitute for professional financial advice, diagnosis, or treatment.

Always seek the advice of your financial advisor, accountant, or other qualified financial professionals with any questions you may have regarding your financial situation or any financial instruments discussed in this book.

The strategies and techniques outlined in this book are based on the author's personal experiences and research. Individual results may vary, and the techniques mentioned may not be suitable for every individual or situation. The reader is advised to conduct their own thorough research and consult with their financial advisor before making any financial decisions.

The author and publisher make no representations or warranties of any kind, express or implied, about the completeness, accuracy, reliability, suitability,

Table of Contents

Foreword

Many of you find yourselves buried in debt, wondering how you can possibly dig yourselves out of this financial shithole. It's a question that plagues millions of people in today's world, where traditional job security is rapidly vanishing, and the pressures of globalization and technological advancement are intensifying. You might feel trapped, but there is a way out. The secret lies in not just getting out of debt but in using debt as a powerful tool to build wealth.

In "Debt to Wealth: Mastering Financial Leverage," we explore the transformative potential of debt. Far from being a burden, debt can be a strategic instrument for financial growth—if you know how to use it wisely. This book will guide you through the principles and practices of leveraging debt to turn your financial situation around.

We'll delve into the essential skills and mindset required to transform debt from a burden into a stepping stone toward financial freedom.

Understanding the broader economic context is crucial. The concept of job security is becoming increasingly obsolete. Globalization has outsourced many blue-collar jobs, and now, with the rise of artificial intelligence and robotics, even white-collar professions are under threat. This rapidly changing job market means that relying solely on traditional employment is no longer a viable strategy for most people.

The United States is in a massive money hole, with the national debt reaching unprecedented levels. As of early 2024, America's national debt has permanently crossed the $34 trillion mark, with each citizen effectively carrying a $1,000,000 share of this debt. This situation has arisen from decades of budget deficits, extensive government spending on essential programs, and economic crises such as the COVID-19 pandemic.

The challenge of managing and eventually reducing this debt is daunting, but understanding its implications and how to navigate it is crucial.

Wealthy individuals and savvy investors have long understood that debt, when used strategically, can be a powerful tool for building wealth. Leveraging debt involves borrowing money at lower interest rates to invest in opportunities that yield higher returns. This practice is common in real estate and stock market investments, where the potential for significant returns can far outweigh the cost of borrowing. By using debt wisely, you can amplify your investment returns and achieve financial growth that would be impossible through savings alone.

Traditional savings strategies are losing their effectiveness in the current financial landscape. With low interest rates on savings accounts and inflation eroding purchasing power, money sitting idle in a bank account is essentially losing value over time.

In contrast, strategic use of debt can lead to financial growth, as borrowing to invest can generate returns that outpace inflation and savings interest rates.

This new financial paradigm challenges the conventional wisdom that saving is the best path to financial security.

Debt, in the modern financial system, essentially functions as money. When the government borrows, it injects money into the economy, stimulating growth and creating opportunities.

For individuals, understanding this concept is crucial. Wealthy people use debt as a tax-free source of funds, allowing them to invest and grow their wealth without incurring the same tax liabilities as traditional income. This approach to debt and investment can significantly enhance financial stability and growth.

The U.S. dollar has, in many ways, become synonymous with debt. As the country accumulates more debt, it simultaneously increases the money supply.

This relationship between debt and currency is a cornerstone of modern economic policy, helping to finance government spending and stimulate economic activity.
For citizens, this means that understanding and utilizing debt is increasingly essential for financial success.

Wealthy individuals and businesses are adept at using debt to their advantage. They borrow to invest in high-yield opportunities, benefiting from tax breaks on interest payments and leveraging their investments to generate significant returns.

This practice contributes to the increasing wealth gap, as those who understand and use debt effectively can grow their wealth much faster than those who rely solely on traditional savings methods.

Learning to use debt effectively is a game-changer for many. It involves understanding the risks and rewards of borrowing, choosing investments wisely, and managing debt responsibly.

Financial education plays a crucial role in this process, empowering individuals to leverage debt for wealth creation rather than falling into the trap of high-interest consumer debt.

One of the significant advantages of debt is that it can be a tax-free source of funds. Unlike income, which is subject to taxes, borrowed money is not taxed. This allows individuals to use debt to finance investments and expenditures without the same tax burden, making it a powerful tool for wealth management and growth.

While America's national debt is a complex and often concerning issue, it also highlights the evolving nature of money and finance. Understanding how debt can be used to build wealth, the limitations of traditional savings strategies, and the benefits of leveraging debt is essential for financial success in today's economy.

By embracing the strategic use of debt, individuals can navigate the challenges of the modern financial landscape and turn potential

liabilities into opportunities for growth and prosperity.
You will gain the knowledge and tools to leverage debt effectively.
Learn about different financial instruments, strategies for managing and reducing debt, and ways to use debt to invest in high-return opportunities.

Readers will have a comprehensive understanding of how to transform debt from a burden into a powerful tool for financial growth and stability.

Welcome to the journey of mastering financial leverage. Together, we will explore the strategies and insights needed to thrive in an era of economic uncertainty and achieve lasting financial success.

Introduction

America is facing an enormous financial challenge: each citizen effectively carries a $1,000,000 share of the national debt. This staggering figure might seem alarming, but it's essential to understand the implications of this debt on individual financial health and the broader economy.

Surprisingly, debt plays a crucial role in making some Americans richer, challenging the conventional wisdom that saving is the best financial strategy. Here's a breakdown of how this massive debt impacts us all and why debt, paradoxically, can be a tool for wealth creation.

The Reality of America's Debt

As of early 2024, the U.S. national debt has soared to over $34 trillion, with the Treasury Department reporting this milestone crossing in January. This debt accumulation stems from decades of budget deficits, high government spending on essential programs like Medicare,

Medicaid, and Social Security, as well as responses to economic crises such as the COVID-19 pandemic. Interest payments alone on this debt are reaching staggering figures, contributing significantly to the national deficit.

Debt as a Wealth-Building Tool

While it may seem counterintuitive, debt can be a powerful tool for building wealth. Wealthy individuals and savvy investors often use debt to their advantage, leveraging it to generate income and grow their assets.

This practice, known as leveraging, involves borrowing money at a lower interest rate to invest in opportunities that yield a higher return. This strategy can significantly amplify returns on investment, a tactic commonly employed in real estate and stock market investments.

Savers Are Losers: The New Financial Paradigm

In the current financial landscape, traditional savings strategies are losing their effectiveness.

With interest rates on savings accounts remaining low and inflation eroding purchasing power, money sitting in a bank account is losing value over time.

On the other hand, debt used strategically can lead to financial growth. By borrowing to invest, individuals can generate returns that outpace inflation and savings interest rates, effectively making savers the real losers in today's economy.

Debt is Money: Understanding the Modern Financial System

In the modern financial system, debt essentially functions as money. When the government borrows, it injects money into the economy, which can stimulate growth and create opportunities.

For individuals, understanding this concept is crucial. Wealthy people use debt as a tax-free source of funds, allowing them to invest and grow their wealth without incurring the same tax liabilities as traditional income.

The Dollar Becomes Debt

The U.S. dollar, in many ways, has become synonymous with debt. As the country accumulates more debt, it simultaneously increases the money supply. This relationship between debt and currency is a cornerstone of modern economic policy, helping to finance government spending and stimulate economic activity. For citizens, this means that understanding and utilizing debt is increasingly essential for financial success.

The Benefits of Debt for the Wealthy

Wealthy individuals and businesses are adept at using debt to their advantage. They borrow to invest in high-yield opportunities, benefiting from tax breaks on interest payments and leveraging their investments to generate significant returns. This practice contributes to the increasing wealth gap, as those who understand and use debt effectively can grow their wealth much faster than those who rely solely on traditional savings methods.

Learning to Use Debt

For many, learning to use debt effectively is a game-changer. This involves understanding the risks and rewards of borrowing, choosing investments wisely, and managing debt responsibly.

Financial education plays a crucial role in this process, empowering individuals to leverage debt for wealth creation rather than falling into the trap of high-interest consumer debt.

Debt is Tax-Free

One of the significant advantages of debt is that it can be a tax-free source of funds. Unlike income, which is subject to taxes, borrowed money is not taxed.

This allows individuals to use debt to finance investments and expenditures without the same tax burden, making it a powerful tool for wealth management and growth.

While America's national debt is a complex and often concerning issue, it also highlights the evolving nature of money and finance.

Understanding how debt can be used to build wealth, the limitations of traditional savings strategies, and the benefits of leveraging debt is essential for financial success in today's economy.

By embracing the strategic use of debt, individuals can navigate the challenges of the modern financial landscape and turn potential liabilities into opportunities for growth and prosperity.

Chapter 1: The Reality of America's Debt

America's financial landscape is dominated by a staggering figure: the national debt, which, as of early 2024, has surpassed $34 trillion.

This debt means each citizen carries an effective share of $1,000,000. The implications of this debt are profound, impacting individual financial health and the broader economy.

Understanding how this debt has accumulated and what it means for the average American is crucial for navigating our financial future.

Streamline the History of U.S. National Debt.

The history of America's national debt is a tale of economic crises, wars, and persistent budget deficits. Historically, the U.S. has borrowed money to finance wars, from the Revolutionary War to the World Wars.

Post-World War II, the debt was substantial, but the booming post-war economy and the advent of industrialization helped manage and reduce it.

However, the late 20th and early 21st centuries saw a shift. The Cold War era led to increased military spending, and the Reagan administration's economic policies, which included significant tax cuts and increased defense spending, added to the debt.

Subsequent administrations faced various economic challenges, from the tech bubble burst in the early 2000s to the Great Recession of 2008, each contributing to the national debt.

In recent decades, the financial strategies of both political parties have also influenced the debt.
Republican-led administrations often prioritize tax cuts as a means to stimulate economic growth, which, while reducing government revenue, do not always lead to proportional decreases in spending.

On the other hand, Democratic administrations typically focus on expanding social programs, which increases expenditures without always balancing the revenue needed to cover these new costs.

This bipartisan approach to governance, where each party pushes for its fiscal priorities, has significantly contributed to the accumulation of national debt over the years.

Factors Contributing to the Current Debt Level

The current debt level results from a combination of factors.
Decades of budget deficits, where government expenditures surpass revenues, have been a significant driver. Government spending on essential programs like Medicare, Medicaid, and Social Security is a substantial portion of the budget.

These programs provide vital services to millions of Americans but are costly to maintain.

Additionally, economic crises such as the COVID-19 pandemic necessitated massive government intervention. Stimulus packages, unemployment benefits, and business support measures were critical in preventing an economic collapse but came at the cost of increased borrowing.

The Treasury Department had to issue more bonds to finance these expenditures, pushing the debt higher.

The increasing costs of healthcare and the aging population also strain the budget. As baby boomers retire, more individuals become eligible for Social Security and Medicare, further driving up government spending.

Healthcare costs in the United States are among the highest in the world, and as these costs continue to rise, so does the government's financial burden.

Interest payments on existing debt also contribute significantly.

As the debt grows, so do the interest payments, creating a cycle where more borrowing is needed to cover these costs. In 2022, interest payments alone were around $400 billion, a figure expected to rise as interest rates increase. This interest burden limits the government's ability to invest in other critical areas such as education, infrastructure, and research and development.

Impact of Government Spending and Economic Crises

Government spending plays a dual role. On one hand, it provides essential services, stimulates economic growth, and supports citizens during crises. On the other hand, excessive spending without adequate revenue leads to budget deficits and increased borrowing.

The COVID-19 pandemic exemplified this. Government spending was crucial to keep the economy afloat, providing direct payments to individuals and support for businesses. However, this added trillions to the national debt.

Similarly, the Great Recession required significant government intervention to stabilize the financial system and stimulate recovery, further increasing the debt.

Military spending is another significant contributor. The U.S. maintains one of the largest defense budgets in the world, funding everything from active military operations to veterans' benefits. While necessary for national security, this spending adds to the fiscal burden.

Education funding, public infrastructure projects, and other essential services also require substantial investment. Balancing these needs with fiscal responsibility is a continual challenge for policymakers.

Education is a critical area where investment is necessary for long-term economic growth, yet funding often falls short due to competing budget priorities. Infrastructure projects, such as repairing aging roads and bridges, are essential for maintaining economic productivity but require significant upfront costs.

Moreover, the political climate influences fiscal policies and spending decisions. Policy gridlocks, where different branches of government are controlled by opposing parties, often lead to delays in budget approvals and inconsistent fiscal policies. These delays can exacerbate economic uncertainties and hinder effective debt management.

Global Context

While the U.S. national debt is significant, it's important to note that many developed nations also face high debt levels. The United States ranks [insert ranking here] among developed countries in terms of national debt to GDP ratio.

Understanding the complexity and multifaceted nature of America's national debt is crucial for developing strategies to manage and mitigate its impact. By examining historical trends, current contributing factors, and the implications of government spending, we can gain a clearer picture of the challenges and potential solutions for America's debt crisis.

The path forward requires not only immediate measures to address the debt but also long-term strategies to ensure sustainable economic growth and fiscal responsibility.

Although it is commonly associated with a negative connotation, debt may be an effective instrument for the development of wealth. When it comes to generating income and expanding their assets, wealthy individuals and astute investors employ debt in a planned manner.

Investing in chances that provide a higher return is an example of the process known as "leveraging," which includes borrowing money at a lower interest rate in order to make investments.

This method has the potential to dramatically increase returns on investment, which is why it is a preferred approach in the process of investing in real estate and the stock market.

A Conceptualization of the Leverage of Debt

The term "leveraging debt" refers to the practice of investing borrowed funds in assets that are anticipated to yield returns that are greater than the cost of borrowing the funds. If you are able to borrow money at a low interest rate and then invest that money in something that offers a greater rate of return, then you will be able to profit from the difference in the interest rates throughout the course of the investment.

For instance, if you take out a loan with an interest rate of 4% and invest in real estate that appreciates at 8% yearly, you will effectively get a return of 4% on the money that you borrowed when you invest in real estate.

You are able to control a significantly larger quantity of capital using this technique than you would be able to with your own money alone, which results in an increase in the possible returns you could receive.

Making sure that the returns on the investment are higher than the cost of the debt, which includes interest payments and any other costs associated with the debt, is the most important factor in achieving successful leverage.

In the realm of leverage, one of the most essential notions is the utilization of "good debt" as opposed to "bad debt." Obtaining assets that will either create income or appreciate over time, such as real estate, stocks, or a business, can be accomplished through the utilization of good debt.

Bad debt, on the other hand, is used to acquire things that lose value over time, such as automobiles or consumer goods, and so does not contribute to the accumulation of wealth.

One must have a solid understanding of this dichotomy in order to make good use of debt in order to generate wealth.

How People Who Are Already Wealthy Make Use of Debt to Generate Income

Individuals who are wealthy are aware of the power that comes with leveraging debt.

Frequently, they make use of mortgages in order to invest in real estate properties, which can both generate rental income and increase in value over time.

By taking out loans to finance these investments, they are able to acquire a greater number of properties and increase their wealth at a faster rate than they would be able to if they relied entirely on their own funding.

The rental income that is generated from these properties can be sufficient to cover the mortgage payments and other obligations, leaving a profit that can be reinvestment in new properties or other options for investment.

Margin loans are a frequent instrument that are utilized in the stock market.

Borrowing money allows investors to purchase more stocks than they would be able to with their own cash alone, which in turn increases their returns when the market is performing well. Although it is a dangerous approach, if it is managed properly, it has the potential to result in significant rewards.

The portfolios of wealthy investors are frequently diversified in order to minimize the risk of loss and enhance the possibility for gain.

They are able to invest in a diversified portfolio of stocks by borrowing money, which allows them to take advantage of chances in the market and obtain larger returns than they would have if they had invested only their own money.

It is also possible for rich people to use debt by taking out loans for their businesses. It is common practice for business owners and entrepreneurs to take out loans in order to launch or expand their companies.

Through the utilization of debt as a means of financing growth, they are able to raise both the revenue and profitability of their business.

A cycle of growth and wealth accumulation can be created by using the additional money earned to repay the loan and invest in further expansion. This will create a cycle of growth and accumulation.

Case Studies: Investments in Real Estate and the Stock Market Real Estate:

Consider the case of a real estate investor who spends $500,000 on the acquisition of a rental property. They put down $100,000 of their own money and then take out a mortgage for the remaining $400,000 at a rate of interest of 4% over the entire loan.

The annual rental income generated by the property is thirty thousand dollars, whereas the annual expenses incurred by the investor, which include mortgage payments, total to twenty-four thousand dollars. As a result, the net income from rentals comes to $6,000.

In addition, the property increases in value at a yearly rate of 5% on average, which results in an annual price increase of $25,000 for the property.

By the end of the first year, the investor has made a return of 31% on their initial investment of $100,000, which is equivalent to $31,000 ($6,000 in rental income plus $25,000 in appreciation).

An illustration of how the utilization of debt can greatly increase returns on real estate investments is provided by this hypothetical scenario.

Investors in real estate also enjoy the benefits of favorable tax treatment. Rental income can be reduced by the investor's ability to deduct expenses like as mortgage interest, property taxes, and depreciation, so lowering the investor's taxable income.

The profitability of real estate investments is further increased as a result of these deductions, which also make the strategy of leveraging debt an even more appealing option.

Market for Stocks:

In order to purchase extra shares on the stock market, an investor may make use of a margin loan at times. Imagine that an investor has $50,000 in their possession and decides to invest in stocks by borrowing another $50,000 at a 6% interest rate.

The overall value of the investment will increase to $110,000 if the stock portfolio experiences a 10% appreciation over the course of a year. Following the repayment of the loan plus interest, which totaled $53,000, the investor is left with $57,000.

This represents a profit of $7,000 on their initial investment of $50,000, which is equivalent to a return of 14%.
A return of only 10% would have been achieved if leverage had not been utilized.

Although margin investing has the potential to yield substantial profits, it also entails a large amount of risk.

In the event that the stock market has a drop, the losses will also be compounded, and the investor may be subject to a margin call, which would require them to either sell assets or deposit additional funds in order to cover the loan.

Since this is the case, it is imperative that investors properly manage their margin accounts and establish stop-loss orders in order to limit the amount of possible losses they could incur.

The Expansion of Small Businesses:

Leveraging debt is another practical use that may be utilized in the process of establishing a small business.

Consider the following scenario: a proprietor of a small business is interested in opening a new location and need $200,000 to cover the costs associated with doing so. In order to finance this sum, they make the decision to obtain a business loan with an interest rate of 5%.

The new site brings in an additional $300,000 in annual income, while the operational expenses amount to $250,000, which results in a net profit of $50,000.

An annual interest payment of $10,000 is required to be made on the loan, which results in a net gain of $40,000 for the owner once the loan installments have been made. This gives a return of twenty percent on the money that was borrowed.

When the owner of a firm uses debt to leverage their expansion, they are able to develop more rapidly than they would be able to if they waited to save the necessary money. This results in increased growth and profitability.

The Investments Made in Education:

Investments in educational opportunities might also be considered a type of debt leverage. A substantial number of professionals obtain student loans in order to fund advanced degrees or certifications that have the potential to dramatically boost their earning potential.

As an illustration, a nurse who takes out a loan of $50,000 in order to earn a master's degree in nursing can see a twenty thousand dollar gain in their annual earnings. The original loan and interest payments are significantly outweighed by this additional income, which amounts to $400,000 over the course of a career spanning twenty years.

Individuals have the ability to improve their skills and qualifications through the utilization of student loans, which can result in higher-paying positions and increased earnings over the course of their lifetime.

An further method by which debt can be deliberately utilized to build wealth is through the investment in human capital.

When it comes to Leveraging Debt, Both Risks and Rewards

Leveraging debt can increase yields, but it also brings about dangers that must be considered.

The performance of leveraged investments can be impacted by a variety of factors, including fluctuations in the market, shifts in interest rates, and economic downturns.
To be successful as an investor, it is essential to have a sound risk management strategy in place and to have a solid understanding of these risks.

When it comes to risk management, diversification is an essential strategy. When investors diversify their holdings over a variety of asset classes and industries, they are able to mitigate the negative effects of the underperformance of any one particular investment.
In times of uncertainty, it is beneficial to have a financial cushion that can be provided by maintaining an emergency fund and having a clear repayment plan for money that have been borrowed.

Because leverage magnifies both gains and losses, it is vital to employ it prudently and within one's risk tolerance in order to maximize one's potential returns.

Investors are able to efficiently use debt to generate wealth if they properly evaluate investment opportunities, have a thorough awareness of the costs of borrowing, and put risk management methods into action.

It is possible to develop wealth through the strategic utilization of debt, which can be a strong instrument. The use of debt by wealthy individuals and astute investors to increase their returns, whether through the purchase of real estate, investments in the stock market, or the expansion of businesses, is a common practice.

For the purpose of successfully utilizing debt as a vehicle for wealth creation, it is essential to have a solid understanding of the notion of leverage, to effectively manage risks, and to make well-informed investment decisions.

When individuals perceive their debt not as a burden but rather as a possible ally in the process of financial progress, they are able to open up new prospects for the production of wealth.

Education, careful preparation, and methodical execution are the means by which success can be achieved. When approached in the appropriate manner, debt has the potential to turn from a difficulty in terms of finances into a potent engine for wealth.

Chapter 2: Debt as a Wealth-Building Tool

Financial intelligence is the cornerstone of effective debt management and wealth creation. It involves understanding how money works, making informed financial decisions, and developing habits that contribute to long-term financial stability.

For now , we will explore the components of financial intelligence, the importance of financial education, and practical steps to enhance your financial IQ.

Developing a Solid Financial Foundation
To build financial intelligence, it is essential to start with a solid foundation. This includes understanding basic financial concepts such as budgeting, saving, investing, and managing debt.
A strong financial foundation enables you to make informed decisions and avoid common financial pitfalls.

Budgeting

Budgeting is the process of creating a plan for how you will spend and save your money. It involves tracking your income and expenses, setting spending limits, and ensuring that you live within your means.
A well-crafted budget helps you allocate resources effectively, prioritize financial goals, and avoid unnecessary debt.

Saving

Saving is a critical aspect of financial intelligence. It involves setting aside a portion of your income for future needs and emergencies.

A healthy savings habit provides a financial cushion that can help you navigate unexpected expenses and opportunities.
Aim to save at least 20% of your income, and build an emergency fund that covers three to six months of living expenses.

Investing

Investing is the process of putting your money to work to generate returns over time. It involves purchasing assets such as stocks, bonds, real estate, and mutual funds that have the potential to appreciate in value or generate income.
Investing wisely requires understanding the risks and rewards associated with different investment options and developing a diversified portfolio that aligns with your financial goals.

Managing Debt

Effective debt management is crucial for financial stability. It involves understanding the terms and conditions of your loans, making timely payments, and prioritizing high-interest debt repayment. Managing debt responsibly helps you maintain a healthy credit score and avoid financial stress.

Cultivating Discipline and Strategic Thinking
Financial intelligence also involves cultivating discipline and strategic thinking.

Making informed financial decisions requires careful planning, self-control, and a long-term perspective.

Setting Financial Goals

Setting clear financial goals provides direction and motivation for managing your finances. Goals can be short-term (e.g., saving for a vacation), medium-term (e.g., buying a car), or long-term (e.g., saving for retirement).

Ensure that your goals are specific, measurable, achievable, relevant, and time-bound (SMART).

Developing Good Financial Habits

Good financial habits are the building blocks of financial intelligence. These include living within your means, saving regularly, avoiding impulsive spending, and staying informed about your financial situation.
Developing these habits requires consistency and self-discipline.

Thinking Strategically

Strategic thinking involves evaluating your financial options, assessing risks, and making decisions that align with your long-term goals. It requires a deep understanding of financial principles and the ability to anticipate and adapt to changing economic conditions. Strategic thinkers are proactive, rather than reactive, in managing their finances.

Financial Education:
The Key to Financial Intelligence
Financial education is the key to building and enhancing financial intelligence. It involves learning about various financial concepts, tools, and strategies, and applying this knowledge to your personal financial situation.

Learning Resources

There are numerous resources available to help you enhance your financial education, including books, online courses, webinars, podcasts, and financial blogs.

Some recommended books include "Rich Dad Poor Dad" by Robert Kiyosaki,
 "The Total Money Makeover" by Dave Ramsey, and "Your Money or Your Life" by Vicki Robin and Joe Dominguez.
Online platforms such as Coursera, Udemy, and Khan Academy offer courses on personal finance and investing.

Seeking Professional Advice

Working with financial advisors, accountants, and other financial professionals can provide valuable insights and guidance. These experts can help you develop a comprehensive financial plan, make informed investment decisions, and navigate complex financial situations.

Staying Informed

Keeping up with financial news and trends is essential for making informed decisions.

Follow reputable financial news sources such as The Wall Street Journal, Bloomberg, and CNBC.

Staying informed about economic developments, market trends, and changes in financial regulations helps you anticipate opportunities and challenges.

Practical Financial Tools
Using practical financial tools can enhance your financial intelligence and simplify money management.
These tools include budgeting apps, investment platforms, and financial calculators.

Budgeting Apps

Budgeting apps such as Mint, YNAB (You Need A Budget), and PocketGuard help you track your income and expenses, set financial goals, and monitor your progress.

These apps provide a clear picture of your financial situation and help you stay on track with your budget.

Investment Platforms

Online investment platforms such as Robinhood, E*TRADE, and Vanguard make it easy to invest in stocks, bonds, and other securities. These platforms offer tools and resources to help you research investments, build a diversified portfolio, and monitor your performance.

Financial Calculators

Financial calculators can help you estimate loan payments, calculate compound interest, and plan for retirement. Websites such as Bankrate and NerdWallet offer a variety of financial calculators to assist with different aspects of financial planning.

Case Studies: Building Financial Intelligence

Case Study 1: Budgeting and Saving

Emily, a 30-year-old marketing manager, struggled with managing her finances. She often found herself overspending and living paycheck to paycheck.

To regain control, Emily started using a budgeting app to track her income and expenses.

She set clear financial goals, including building an emergency fund and saving for a down payment on a house. By sticking to her budget and prioritizing saving, Emily was able to improve her financial situation significantly. She now has a solid emergency fund and is on track to achieve her homeownership goal.

Case Study 2: Investing for the Future

Michael, a 45-year-old software engineer, realized he needed to start investing to secure his financial future. He began by educating himself about different investment options through books and online courses. Michael opened an account with an online investment platform and started building a diversified portfolio of stocks, bonds, and mutual funds. By regularly contributing to his investments and reinvesting dividends, Michael has seen his portfolio grow steadily over the years. His strategic approach to investing has put him on a path to financial security in retirement.

Case Study 3: Managing Debt

Rachel, a 35-year-old nurse, was struggling with high-interest credit card debt. She decided to take control of her finances by consolidating her debt into a lower-interest personal loan. Rachel created a detailed repayment plan and prioritized paying off her debt aggressively. She also adopted better financial habits, such as living within her means and avoiding unnecessary credit card use. As a result, Rachel was able to pay off her debt within a few years and significantly improve her credit score. Her experience taught her the importance of effective debt management and financial discipline.

Conclusion
Building financial intelligence is a critical step towards achieving financial success and leveraging debt effectively. By developing a solid financial foundation, cultivating discipline and strategic thinking, and enhancing your financial education, you can make informed decisions that contribute to long-term financial stability and growth.

As you continue this journey, remember that financial intelligence is not a destination but a continuous process of learning and improvement. Embrace the principles and practices discussed in this chapter, and use them as a foundation for the strategies and insights explored in the following chapters of "Debt to Wealth: Mastering Financial Leverage."

In the next chapter, we will delve into effective debt management strategies, exploring techniques for assessing your debt situation, prioritizing repayments, and utilizing financial instruments to consolidate and manage debt. With a strong foundation of financial intelligence, you will be well-equipped to navigate the complexities of debt and transform it into a tool for wealth creation.

Chapter 3: Savers Are Losers: The New Financial Paradigm

In today's financial landscape, the traditional strategy of saving money in a bank account is no longer the effective path to wealth it once was. With historically low-interest rates on savings accounts and rising inflation, traditional savings strategies are not just ineffective; they can actually lead to a loss in purchasing power. This chapter delves into why conventional savings methods are failing and explores how leveraging debt and investing can provide a more robust path to financial growth and stability.

The Ineffectiveness of Traditional Savings Strategies
For many years, people have been taught that saving money in a bank account is a safe and effective way to build wealth. This belief was based on the notion that money in a savings account would grow over time due to compound interest.

However, in the current economic environment, this strategy is no longer viable.

Interest rates on savings accounts have been near historic lows for over a decade. According to the Federal Deposit Insurance Corporation (FDIC), the average interest rate on savings accounts in the United States has been below 1% for many years. At the same time, inflation rates have been rising, often outpacing the returns on savings accounts. This means that the real value of money saved in these accounts is decreasing over time.

The Impact of Low Interest Rates and Inflation To understand why traditional savings strategies are ineffective, it's essential to examine the impact of low-interest rates and inflation. Central banks, such as the Federal Reserve, often lower interest rates to stimulate economic growth by making borrowing cheaper. While this can boost economic activity, it also means that savers earn very little on their deposits.

Inflation further compounds this issue. Inflation is the rate at which the general level of prices for goods and services rises, eroding purchasing power. When the inflation rate exceeds the interest rate on savings accounts, the real return on savings is negative. For example, if the inflation rate is 3% and a savings account yields 1%, the real return is -2%. Over time, this negative return can significantly diminish the value of savings.

The New Financial Paradigm: Investing Over Saving

In response to these challenges, a new financial paradigm is emerging. Instead of relying on traditional savings accounts, individuals are increasingly turning to investments to grow their wealth. Investing allows money to work for you, generating returns that can outpace inflation and low-interest rates.

The Power of Compound Interest
One of the most compelling reasons to invest is the power of compound interest.

Compound interest occurs when the interest earned on an investment is reinvested, generating additional earnings over time. This creates a snowball effect, where the investment grows exponentially. For example, investing $10,000 at an average annual return of 7% will grow to $19,671 in ten years, significantly outpacing the returns from a traditional savings account.

Diversification to Manage Risk

Investing inherently involves risk, but diversification can help manage that risk. Diversification means spreading investments across various asset classes, such as stocks, bonds, real estate, and alternative investments.

By not putting all your eggs in one basket, you can reduce the impact of poor performance in any single asset. A diversified portfolio can provide more stable and consistent returns over time, helping to mitigate the risks associated with investing.

Risk Management Strategies

While acknowledging investment risks, it's crucial to delve deeper into risk management strategies such as diversification and asset allocation. Diversification involves spreading investments across different asset classes, sectors, and geographic regions to reduce exposure to any single risk. Asset allocation refers to the strategy of dividing an investment portfolio among different asset categories, such as stocks, bonds, and real estate, based on an investor's risk tolerance and time horizon. By employing these strategies, investors can manage risk more effectively and achieve more balanced returns.

Leveraging Debt for Investment
Strategically using debt to invest can amplify your returns. This involves borrowing money at a lower interest rate and investing it in opportunities that offer higher returns. For instance, taking out a mortgage to buy rental properties can provide rental income and property appreciation, potentially yielding a return greater than the cost of the mortgage.

Similarly, margin loans in the stock market allow you to borrow money to buy more stocks, increasing your potential returns. However, it's important to understand and manage the risks associated with leveraging debt.

Debt Risks and Responsibilities
While leveraging debt can amplify returns, it also comes with significant risks and responsibilities. It's essential to use debt responsibly and understand the potential pitfalls. Bad debt, such as high-interest credit card debt or payday loans, can quickly become unmanageable and lead to financial ruin. It's crucial to maintain a healthy debt-to-income ratio and avoid overleveraging. This means borrowing within your means and ensuring that debt repayments are manageable within your budget.

Investment Options and Considerations
Investors have various options to choose from, each with its own risk-reward profile. Here's a brief overview of different investment options:

Stocks: Investing in individual stocks offers high potential returns but comes with higher risk. Diversification and market awareness are key to managing this risk.

Bonds: Bonds are generally safer investments that provide regular interest payments but offer lower returns compared to stocks.

Real Estate: Real estate investments can generate steady income and appreciate over time, but they require strategic property selection and management.

Mutual Funds and ETFs: These funds pool money from many investors to buy a diversified portfolio of stocks, bonds, or other securities, offering diversification and professional management.

Alternative Investments: These include commodities, private equity, hedge funds, and cryptocurrencies. They can provide high returns but also come with high risk and complexity.

Comparing Savings vs. Investment Returns

To illustrate the difference between saving and investing, let's compare the potential returns:

Scenario 1: Savings Account

Initial amount: $10,000
Annual interest rate: 1%
Inflation rate: 3%
After one year: $10,100
Real value after one year: $9,797 (adjusted for inflation)

Scenario 2: Investment Portfolio

Initial amount: $10,000
Average annual return: 7%
Inflation rate: 3%
After one year: $10,700
Real value after one year: $10,388 (adjusted for inflation)

In the savings account scenario, the real value of your money decreases due to inflation. In contrast, the investment portfolio grows, even after adjusting for inflation.

This comparison highlights why investing is increasingly essential for building wealth in today's economic environment.

Embracing a New Financial Mindset
Adopting this new financial paradigm requires a shift in mindset and strategy. Here are key principles to guide this transition:

Invest Regularly and Consistently: Consistency is crucial when it comes to investing. By investing regularly, such as through a monthly contribution to a retirement account or investment portfolio, you can take advantage of dollar-cost averaging. This strategy reduces the impact of market volatility by spreading your investments over time.

Stay Educated and Informed: Financial education is vital for making informed investment decisions. Stay updated on market trends, economic indicators, and investment opportunities. Utilize resources such as financial news, investment courses, and professional advice to enhance your knowledge and skills.

Focus on Long-Term Goals: Investing with a long-term perspective allows you to benefit from the compounding effect and weather short-term market fluctuations. Set clear financial goals and develop a plan to achieve them. Whether saving for retirement, buying a home, or funding education, having a long-term focus helps maintain discipline and patience.

Diversify Your Portfolio: Diversification is key to managing risk and optimizing returns. Spread your investments across different asset classes and industries to reduce the impact of poor performance in any single area. A well-diversified portfolio provides more stable and consistent growth over time.

Use Debt Strategically: Leverage debt judiciously to amplify your investment returns. Understand the risks and rewards of borrowing and use debt to invest in opportunities that offer higher returns than the cost of borrowing. Manage debt responsibly to avoid overleveraging and financial strain.

Real-Life Applications of Debt Strategies

Real Estate Investment: Jane, a middle-income earner, used a mortgage to purchase rental properties. By carefully selecting properties in high-demand areas and managing them efficiently, she generated rental income that exceeded her mortgage payments. Over time, the properties appreciated in value, significantly increasing her net worth.

Stock Market Investment:
John, a tech industry professional, used margin loans to invest in high-growth tech stocks. By diversifying his investments and staying informed about market trends, he achieved substantial returns. Although he experienced some market downturns, his overall strategy led to significant financial gains.

Small Business Expansion:
Lisa, a small business owner, took out a business loan to expand her operations. She invested in new equipment and hired additional staff, increasing her production capacity and revenue.

The increased profits allowed her to repay the loan quickly and continue growing her business.

Practical Steps to Start Investing

Set Clear Financial Goals: Determine what you want to achieve with your investments. Whether it's saving for retirement, buying a home, or funding your children's education, having clear goals will guide your investment decisions.

Create a Budget:
Before you start investing, create a budget to understand your income, expenses, and how much you can afford to invest. Make sure you have an emergency fund in place to cover unexpected expenses.

Choose an Investment Strategy:
Decide on an investment strategy that aligns with your goals and risk tolerance. Consider factors such as your time horizon, financial situation, and investment knowledge.

Start with simple strategies, such as investing in index funds or ETFs, and diversify your portfolio.

Open an Investment Account:
Choose a brokerage or investment platform that meets your needs. Many online brokers offer low fees, user-friendly interfaces, and a wide range of investment options. Robo-advisors can also be a good choice for those seeking a hands-off approach.

Start Small and Be Consistent:
Begin with small investments and gradually increase your contributions as you become more comfortable and knowledgeable. Consistency is key; make regular contributions to your investment account to take advantage of dollar-cost averaging.

Monitor and Adjust Your Portfolio:
Regularly review your investment portfolio to ensure it remains aligned with your goals and risk tolerance. Rebalance your portfolio as needed to maintain your desired asset allocation.

Stay informed about market trends and economic conditions that may impact your investments.

Seek Professional Advice:
If you are unsure about your investment strategy or need guidance, consider seeking advice from a financial advisor. A professional can help you create a personalized investment plan and provide ongoing support.

The financial landscape is evolving, and traditional savings strategies are no longer sufficient for achieving financial success. Low interest rates and rising inflation have eroded the effectiveness of saving money in conventional ways.
To build wealth and secure your financial future, it is essential to embrace a new paradigm that prioritizes investing over saving.

By understanding the limitations of traditional savings methods and leveraging the power of investments, you can grow your wealth more effectively.

This requires a shift in mindset, focusing on long-term goals, diversification, and strategic use of debt. Staying educated and informed about market trends and investment opportunities is crucial for making sound financial decisions.

Chapter 4: Debt is Money: Understanding the Modern Financial System

In the modern financial system, debt plays a crucial role in driving economic activity and growth. While debt is often perceived negatively, understanding its fundamental role in the economy is essential. This chapter explores the concept of debt as money, how government borrowing stimulates growth, and the intricate relationship between debt and currency.

The Role of Debt in the Economy

Debt is a fundamental component of the financial system, serving as a tool for both governments and individuals to finance expenditures and investments. Essentially, debt allows for the allocation of future income to current needs, facilitating economic activity and growth.

Governments borrow money to finance public expenditures, such as infrastructure projects, social programs, and defense. By issuing bonds, the government raises capital from investors, who, in return, receive periodic interest payments and the promise of repayment at a future date. This borrowing enables the government to invest in long-term projects that stimulate economic growth, create jobs, and improve public welfare.

In the private sector, businesses and individuals borrow money for various purposes, such as expanding operations, purchasing homes, or funding education. Access to credit allows businesses to invest in new technologies, increase production, and enter new markets, thereby driving economic growth.

For individuals, debt provides the means to invest in assets that can appreciate over time, such as real estate and education, contributing to personal financial growth and stability.

Debt can also stimulate economic activity by increasing consumer spending.

When individuals and businesses have access to credit, they can spend more on goods and services, driving demand and boosting economic growth. This increased spending can lead to higher production, more jobs, and greater overall economic activity.

How Government Borrowing Stimulates Growth

Government borrowing stimulates economic growth, particularly during periods of economic downturn or crisis. By injecting liquidity into the economy through borrowing, the government can finance critical expenditures and provide relief to businesses and individuals.

During economic recessions, governments often implement fiscal stimulus measures to counteract declining economic activity. These measures can include direct payments to individuals, increased funding for unemployment benefits, and investments in infrastructure projects. By borrowing to finance these expenditures, the government injects money into the economy, increasing aggregate demand and stimulating economic growth.

Government borrowing is often used to finance infrastructure projects, such as building roads, bridges, schools, and hospitals. These projects create jobs, improve public services, and enhance the overall quality of life. Additionally, improved infrastructure can boost productivity and attract private investment, further driving economic growth.

Government borrowing allows for counter-cyclical spending, where the government increases expenditures during economic downturns and reduces spending during periods of economic growth. This approach helps stabilize the economy by smoothing out fluctuations in economic activity. During a recession, increased government spending can offset declining private sector spending, preventing a deeper economic contraction.

Government borrowing is often coordinated with monetary policy to achieve macroeconomic objectives. Central banks, such as the Federal Reserve, may purchase government bonds to increase the money supply and lower interest rates.

This coordination between fiscal and monetary policy can enhance the effectiveness of economic stimulus measures and support overall economic stability.

The Relationship Between Debt and Currency

Debt and currency are closely intertwined in the modern financial system. Understanding this relationship is crucial for comprehending how debt functions as money and its broader implications for the economy.

In the modern financial system, money is created through the process of lending. When banks issue loans, they create new money by crediting the borrower's account with the loan amount.

This process increases the money supply and stimulates economic activity. Government borrowing also contributes to money creation when central banks purchase government bonds, injecting liquidity into the economy.

Debt functions as a form of currency in the financial system. Government bonds, for example, are widely traded financial instruments that serve as a store of value and a medium of exchange.

Investors purchase government bonds with the expectation of receiving interest payments and repayment of the principal, much like depositing money in a savings account. These bonds can be bought and sold in secondary markets, providing liquidity and facilitating financial transactions.

The relationship between debt and currency has significant implications for inflation and interest rates. When the government borrows money, it increases the money supply, which can lead to inflation if the economy is operating at or near full capacity.

Central banks monitor inflation and adjust interest rates to maintain price stability. By raising interest rates, central banks can reduce borrowing and spending, thereby controlling inflation. Conversely, lowering interest rates can encourage borrowing and spending, stimulating economic activity.

The level of government debt can also impact the value of a country's currency. High levels of debt may lead to concerns about a government's ability to repay its obligations, potentially weakening the currency. Conversely, responsible debt management and strong economic growth can enhance investor confidence, supporting the currency's value. Exchange rates are influenced by various factors, including interest rates, inflation, and perceptions of economic stability.

Conclusion

Understanding the role of debt in the modern financial system is crucial for comprehending how economies function and how financial policies impact everyday life.

Debt serves as a vital tool for stimulating economic growth, financing public expenditures, and managing economic stability. However, it also carries significant implications for inflation, taxation, and overall economic health.

"Debt to Wealth: Mastering Financial Leverage" aims to provide readers with the knowledge and tools to navigate the complexities of debt and leverage it for financial growth. By exploring the principles of leveraging debt and understanding the broader economic context, individuals can make informed decisions that contribute to personal financial stability and prosperity.

Embrace this journey, and you will be well-equipped to achieve lasting financial success in an ever-changing economic landscape.

Chapter 5: The Dollar Becomes Debt

In the modern financial landscape, the relationship between debt and money supply is intricate and deeply intertwined. The U.S. dollar, as the world's primary reserve currency, plays a unique role in this dynamic. This chapter explores the connection between debt and money supply, how government spending is financed through debt, and the economic implications for citizens. Understanding these concepts is crucial for grasping the broader economic context and making informed financial decisions.

The Connection Between Debt and Money Supply
In the contemporary financial system, the creation of money is closely linked to the issuance of debt. This relationship is foundational to how modern economies operate, impacting everything from inflation rates to economic growth.

Money Creation Through Lending

One of the primary ways money is created in the modern economy is through the lending activities of commercial banks. When a bank issues a loan, it creates new money by crediting the borrower's account with the loan amount. This process expands the money supply, increasing the total amount of money circulating in the economy.

For example, if a bank provides a mortgage loan of $200,000, it credits the borrower's account with this amount, thereby creating new money. The borrower can then use these funds to purchase a home, injecting money into the real estate market and related sectors. This cycle of lending and spending drives economic activity and growth.

Government Bonds and Money Supply

Government borrowing through the issuance of bonds also plays a critical role in money creation. When the government needs to finance its expenditures beyond its revenues, it issues bonds to raise capital from investors.

These bonds are essentially IOUs, promising to pay back the principal amount along with interest at a future date.

Central banks, such as the Federal Reserve in the United States, can purchase these government bonds, injecting liquidity into the economy.

This process is part of monetary policy, aimed at managing economic activity and controlling inflation. By buying government bonds, central banks increase the money supply, making more money available for lending and investment.

Quantitative Easing
Quantitative easing (QE) is a specific monetary policy tool used by central banks to increase the money supply by purchasing government bonds and other financial assets. This approach was widely used during the global financial crisis of 2008 and the COVID-19 pandemic to provide liquidity to the financial system, lower interest rates, and stimulate economic growth.

Through QE, central banks purchase large quantities of government bonds from financial institutions, providing them with cash that can be used for lending and investment. This injection of liquidity supports economic activity by making borrowing cheaper and encouraging spending. However, QE also carries the risk of inflation if the increased money supply outpaces economic growth.

Financing Government Spending Through Debt
Government spending is often financed through borrowing, allowing for the allocation of resources to various public needs without immediate tax increases. This approach enables governments to invest in long-term projects and provide essential services, but it also raises concerns about fiscal responsibility and debt sustainability.

Budget Deficits
When government expenditures exceed revenues, a budget deficit occurs. To finance this deficit, the government borrows money by issuing bonds.

These bonds are purchased by investors, both domestic and international, who provide the capital needed to fund government spending. Budget deficits can result from various factors, including economic downturns, increased spending on social programs, and emergency expenditures.

For instance, during economic recessions, tax revenues often decline as businesses earn less and unemployment rises.

Simultaneously, government spending on social programs like unemployment benefits and healthcare typically increases. This combination of lower revenues and higher expenditures leads to budget deficits, necessitating borrowing.

Long-Term Investments
Government borrowing allows for long-term investments in infrastructure, education, healthcare, and other critical areas. These investments contribute to economic growth, improve public services, and enhance the quality of life for citizens.

For example, borrowing to build highways, bridges, and public transportation systems can create jobs, reduce transportation costs, and boost economic productivity.

Education funding is another critical area where government borrowing can have a long-term positive impact.

By investing in education, governments can improve the skills and productivity of the workforce, leading to higher economic growth and increased tax revenues in the future.

Economic Stabilization

During economic crises, such as recessions or pandemics, government borrowing can play a vital role in stabilizing the economy.

By borrowing to finance stimulus measures, the government can provide direct financial support to individuals and businesses, preventing deeper economic contractions.

For instance, during the COVID-19 pandemic, governments worldwide implemented massive stimulus packages, including direct payments to citizens and support for businesses, to mitigate the economic impact. These measures helped maintain consumer spending and business operations, preventing a more severe economic downturn.

Counter-Cyclical Fiscal Policy
Government borrowing also enables the implementation of counter-cyclical fiscal policies. During economic booms, governments can reduce borrowing and pay down debt, while during recessions, they can increase borrowing to finance stimulus measures. This approach helps stabilize the economy by smoothing out fluctuations in economic activity.

By increasing spending during economic downturns, governments can offset declines in private sector spending, preventing deeper recessions. Conversely, by reducing spending and borrowing during economic booms, governments can prevent the economy from overheating and control inflation.

Economic Implications for Citizens
Government borrowing and the resulting national debt have significant implications for citizens. Understanding these implications is crucial for making informed financial decisions and advocating for responsible fiscal policies.

Interest Payments
One of the primary concerns with high levels of government debt is the burden of interest payments. As the debt grows, so do the interest payments, which must be financed through taxes or additional borrowing. High interest payments can limit the government's ability to fund essential services and investments, potentially leading to higher taxes or reduced public spending.

For instance, in 2022, the U.S. government spent approximately $400 billion on interest payments for its debt. This amount is expected to rise as the debt increases and interest rates potentially go up. Higher interest payments mean fewer resources are available for other critical areas, such as healthcare, education, and infrastructure.

Inflation and Cost of Living
Excessive government borrowing can lead to inflation if it results in an excessive increase in the money supply. Inflation erodes the purchasing power of money, making goods and services more expensive for consumers. This can have a disproportionate impact on low- and middle-income households, who may struggle to keep up with rising costs.

Inflation also affects interest rates, as central banks may raise rates to control inflation. Higher interest rates can increase borrowing costs for individuals and businesses, potentially slowing economic growth.

Taxation and Public Services
To manage high levels of debt, governments may need to increase taxes or cut public spending. Higher taxes reduce disposable income for individuals and businesses, potentially slowing economic growth. Cuts to public services can impact the quality of education, healthcare, and infrastructure, affecting the overall well-being of citizens.

For example, austerity measures implemented in some countries to manage debt levels have led to significant reductions in public services and social programs, adversely affecting vulnerable populations.

Economic Stability
Responsible debt management is essential for maintaining economic stability. While borrowing can stimulate growth and provide essential services, excessive debt can undermine investor confidence and lead to financial instability. Governments must balance the need for borrowing with fiscal responsibility to ensure long-term economic health.

The Global Role of the U.S. Dollar
The U.S. dollar holds a unique position in the global financial system as the world's primary reserve currency. This status has significant implications for how U.S. debt is perceived and managed.

Reserve Currency Status

As the world's primary reserve currency, the U.S. dollar is held in significant quantities by central banks and financial institutions worldwide. This status provides the U.S. with certain advantages, such as the ability to borrow at lower interest rates and increased demand for U.S. government bonds.

Countries hold U.S. dollars as part of their foreign exchange reserves to facilitate international trade and stabilize their own currencies. This demand for dollars supports the value of the currency and helps keep borrowing costs low for the U.S. government.

Trade and Investment

The U.S. dollar's reserve currency status also impacts global trade and investment. Many commodities, such as oil, are priced in dollars, making it a critical currency for international trade.

Additionally, foreign investors often purchase U.S. assets, such as government bonds and real estate, due to the perceived stability and security of the dollar.

This global demand for dollars and dollar-denominated assets helps support the U.S. economy by providing a steady stream of foreign investment and maintaining the currency's value.

Monetary Policy Influence

The U.S. Federal Reserve's monetary policy decisions have global implications due to the dollar's reserve currency status. Changes in U.S. interest rates can impact capital flows, exchange rates, and economic activity worldwide.
For example, an increase in U.S. interest rates can attract foreign investment, strengthening the dollar and potentially leading to capital outflows from emerging markets.

Conversely, a decrease in U.S. interest rates can weaken the dollar and support global economic growth by making borrowing cheaper and increasing liquidity.

The Future of Debt and Currency

The relationship between debt and currency is likely to continue evolving in response to economic conditions, policy decisions, and technological advancements. Understanding these dynamics is crucial for navigating the complexities of the modern financial system.

Technological Innovations
Technological advancements, such as digital currencies and blockchain technology, have the potential to transform the financial system.

Central banks worldwide are exploring the development of central bank digital currencies (CBDCs) to enhance payment systems and improve monetary policy effectiveness.

Digital currencies could change the way money is created and circulated, potentially reducing reliance on traditional banking systems and altering the dynamics of debt and money supply. However, the widespread adoption of digital currencies also poses challenges, such as cybersecurity risks and regulatory considerations.

Fiscal and Monetary Policy Coordination
Effective coordination between fiscal and monetary policy will remain essential for managing debt and economic stability. Governments and central banks must work together to balance the need for economic stimulus with the risks of inflation and financial instability.

For instance, during economic crises, coordinated efforts between fiscal stimulus measures and monetary policy actions, such as QE, can provide a more comprehensive approach to stabilizing the economy.

Conversely, during periods of economic growth, coordinated efforts to reduce deficits and manage debt levels can help ensure long-term sustainability.

Global Economic Shifts
Global economic shifts, such as changes in trade dynamics, demographic trends, and geopolitical developments, will also influence the relationship between debt and currency. For example, an aging population in many developed countries may increase demand for social services and healthcare, leading to higher government spending and debt.

Geopolitical developments, such as trade tensions and changes in international alliances, can impact global capital flows and demand for reserve currencies. Understanding these shifts and their implications for debt and currency is crucial for navigating the future financial landscape.

The intricate relationship between debt and money supply is a cornerstone of the modern financial system.

Understanding how debt functions as money, the role of government borrowing in financing public expenditures, and the economic implications for citizens is crucial for making informed financial decisions.

Government borrowing allows for critical investments and economic stabilization, but it also carries significant responsibilities and risks.

Managing debt levels and ensuring fiscal responsibility are essential for maintaining economic stability and supporting long-term growth.

As the global financial system continues to evolve, staying informed about the dynamics of debt and currency will be increasingly important.
By leveraging the principles of debt management and investment, individuals can navigate the complexities of the financial landscape and achieve lasting financial success.

"Debt to Wealth: Mastering Financial Leverage" aims to equip readers with the knowledge and tools to understand and harness the power of debt for financial growth. Embrace this journey, and you will be well-prepared to thrive in an ever-changing economic environment.

Chapter 6: The Benefits of Debt for the Wealthy

In contemporary finance, debt is often seen as a tool to be avoided, particularly by those who struggle to manage their finances. However, for the wealthy, debt can be a powerful instrument for wealth creation and financial leverage.

This chapter explores how affluent individuals and businesses use debt to their advantage, leveraging investments for significant returns, and examines the growing wealth gap and its implications.

Tax Breaks and Interest Payments

One of the significant advantages of debt for the wealthy is the tax benefits associated with interest payments. In many tax systems, interest paid on loans for investment purposes can be deducted from taxable income, reducing the overall tax burden.

Mortgage Interest Deduction:
In the United States, for instance, homeowners can deduct the interest paid on their mortgage from their taxable income. This deduction can be substantial, especially for high-income individuals with large mortgages.
By reducing taxable income, the mortgage interest deduction effectively lowers the cost of borrowing.

The impact of this deduction can be illustrated with a simple example. Suppose a high-income individual purchases a luxury home with a mortgage of $2 million at an interest rate of 3.5%.
The annual interest payment would be $70,000. If this individual is in the 37% federal tax bracket, the mortgage interest deduction would reduce their taxable income by $70,000, resulting in a tax saving of $25,900.
This effectively lowers the cost of the mortgage, making it a financially savvy move for those who can afford it.

Investment Loan Interest:
Interest on loans used to purchase investments, such as stocks or real estate, can also be deductible.
This means that wealthy individuals can borrow money to invest and then deduct the interest payments on those loans from their taxable income.
This strategy not only reduces the cost of borrowing but also enhances the net returns on investments.

For example, if an investor takes out a $1 million loan at an interest rate of 4% to purchase real estate and earns an 8% return on the investment, they can deduct the $40,000 in annual interest payments from their taxable income. If they are in a high tax bracket, this deduction can significantly reduce their overall tax liability.

This ability to deduct interest payments effectively lowers the cost of leveraging investments, making it a powerful tool for building wealth.

Debt as Tax-Free Money

Debt can effectively function as tax-free money.
When you borrow money, that amount is not
considered taxable income. Instead, it is a
liability that you are obligated to repay.
This characteristic of debt makes it an attractive
option for financing investments.

Comparison with Equity:
Equity, on the other hand, represents
ownership and is often generated from after-tax
income. For instance, if you earn a salary, it is
subject to income tax, which could be as high as
40% or more in the United States. The
remaining amount is what you have available
for investment. In contrast, borrowed money is
not taxed when you receive it, making it a more
cost-effective way to finance investments.

Interest Payments vs. Dividends:
Interest payments on debt are generally tax-
deductible, which reduces the effective cost of
borrowing. For example, if you borrow $1
million at an interest rate of 5%, the annual
interest payment would be $50,000.

If you can deduct this amount from your taxable income and you are in the 37% tax bracket, the tax saving would be $18,500. This effectively reduces the cost of borrowing to $31,500.

On the other hand, dividends paid on equity are not tax-deductible. If a company issues equity to raise funds, it must pay dividends to shareholders from its after-tax profits.

This makes equity a more expensive option compared to debt, as the cost of capital for equity includes the tax on earnings before dividends can be distributed.

Leveraging Investments for Significant Returns

The wealthy often use debt to leverage their investments, amplifying potential returns. This strategy involves borrowing money at a lower interest rate to invest in assets that are expected to generate higher returns.
While leveraging can increase both gains and losses, it is a common tactic among affluent investors who can manage the associated risks.

Real Estate Investments:
Real estate is a popular asset class for leveraging. Wealthy individuals and businesses often use mortgages to finance property purchases, allowing them to control valuable assets with relatively little of their own capital. Rental income and property appreciation can generate substantial returns, often exceeding the cost of borrowing.

Consider a real estate investor who purchases a $5 million commercial property with a $1 million down payment and a $4 million mortgage at an interest rate of 3.5%. If the property generates $400,000 in annual rental income and appreciates by 5% per year, the investor's return on equity can be significantly higher than if they had purchased the property outright. The rental income covers the mortgage payments, and the appreciation increases the property's value, enhancing the investor's overall return.

In addition to rental income and appreciation, real estate investments offer other financial benefits, such as depreciation deductions.

Depreciation allows investors to deduct a portion of the property's value from their taxable income each year, further reducing their tax liability. These combined benefits make real estate a powerful tool for wealth creation when leveraged effectively.

Stock Market Investments:
Margin loans are another way the wealthy leverage investments. By borrowing money to purchase stocks, investors can increase their exposure to the market and potentially achieve higher returns. However, margin investing also carries higher risk, as losses can be magnified in a market downturn.

Consider an investor with a $1 million portfolio who borrows an additional $500,000 at an interest rate of 5% to purchase more stocks. If the stock portfolio appreciates by 10%, the investor earns $150,000 on their $1.5 million investment. After paying $25,000 in interest, the net gain is $125,000, representing a 12.5% return on the initial $1 million, compared to a 10% return without leverage.

While the potential for higher returns is attractive, margin investing requires careful risk management. Market volatility can lead to significant losses, especially if the value of the stocks falls below the loan amount.

Wealthy investors often mitigate this risk by diversifying their portfolios and using stop-loss orders to limit potential losses.

Private Equity and Venture Capital:
Wealthy individuals often invest in private equity and venture capital, which involve providing capital to private companies in exchange for equity ownership.
These investments can offer high returns, particularly if the companies experience significant growth or are acquired. Leveraging debt to finance these investments can enhance returns, although the risks are also higher compared to traditional investments.

Private equity investments typically involve purchasing a significant stake in a company and working to improve its operations and profitability.

This hands-on approach can lead to substantial returns when the company is eventually sold or goes public.

Venture capital, on the other hand, involves investing in early-stage companies with high growth potential.

While the risks are greater, successful venture capital investments can yield returns many times the initial investment.

For example, consider a venture capitalist who invests $1 million in a startup with high growth potential. To finance the investment, they take out a $500,000 loan at an interest rate of 6%.

If the startup grows rapidly and is acquired for $10 million, the venture capitalist's equity stake could be worth $5 million.

After repaying the loan and interest, the net return on the initial investment is significantly enhanced.

The Growing Wealth Gap and Its Implications

The strategic use of debt by the wealthy contributes to the growing wealth gap.

As affluent individuals and businesses leverage debt to enhance their returns, they can accumulate wealth at a much faster rate than those who rely solely on their own capital or traditional savings methods.

Income and Wealth Disparity:
Income and wealth disparity have been increasing globally, with a significant portion of wealth concentrated among the top 1% of earners.
The ability to use debt effectively is a key factor in this disparity.

While middle- and lower-income individuals often use debt for consumption, such as credit card debt or auto loans, the wealthy use debt to invest in appreciating assets.

This disparity is evident in the types of debt held by different income groups. According to data from the Federal Reserve, higher-income households are more likely to hold mortgage debt and investment loans, while lower-income households are more likely to carry credit card debt and personal loans.

The former types of debt are used to acquire assets that can appreciate and generate income, while the latter often finance consumption and do not contribute to wealth building.

Economic Mobility:
The growing wealth gap has implications for economic mobility. Those with access to capital and financial knowledge can leverage debt to create more wealth, while those without such access may struggle to build financial security. This disparity can lead to reduced social and economic mobility, where the wealthy have more opportunities to invest in education, business ventures, and other wealth-building activities.

For example, access to education is a significant factor in economic mobility. Wealthy families can afford to send their children to prestigious schools and universities, providing them with valuable skills and networks. In contrast, lower-income families may struggle to afford higher education, limiting their children's opportunities for upward mobility.

Policy Considerations:
Addressing the wealth gap requires thoughtful policy interventions. Policies that promote financial education, access to credit for small businesses, and affordable housing can help bridge the gap. Additionally, tax policies that encourage investment in underserved communities and provide incentives for wealth-building activities among lower- and middle-income individuals can promote more equitable economic growth.

For instance, policies that support affordable housing initiatives can help lower-income families build equity through homeownership. Programs that provide grants or low-interest loans to small businesses can enable entrepreneurs to start or expand their businesses, creating jobs and stimulating economic growth.
Financial education programs can empower individuals to make informed decisions about debt and investment, helping them build wealth over time.

Social Implications:
The growing wealth gap also has social implications. Economic inequality can lead to social unrest, decreased trust in institutions, and increased political polarization. Addressing these issues requires a comprehensive approach that includes economic, educational, and social policies aimed at creating a more inclusive and equitable society.

For example, economic inequality can lead to social tensions as those who feel left behind become frustrated with the lack of opportunities.
This frustration can manifest in various forms, including protests and political movements advocating for change. Building a more inclusive society requires addressing the root causes of inequality and creating pathways for economic mobility for all individuals.

Debt can be a powerful wealth-building tool when used strategically. By understanding tax advantages, leveraging investments, and managing risks, individuals can use debt to achieve financial growth and stability.

Financial education and informed decision-making are essential for navigating the complexities of debt and leveraging it for financial success.

"Debt to Wealth: Mastering Financial Leverage" aims to provide readers with the knowledge and tools to navigate the complexities of debt and leverage it for financial success.

Embrace this journey, and you will be well-prepared to thrive in an ever-changing economic environment.

Chapter 7: Learning To Use Debt

Debt can be a powerful tool for wealth creation, but it requires careful handling to avoid pitfalls. This chapter equips you with the knowledge to leverage debt effectively, balancing risks and rewards to achieve financial growth and stability.

Weighing the Risks and Rewards

Rewards: Access to Capital

Debt provides access to capital that can be used to invest in income-generating or appreciating assets. When managed wisely, this can significantly amplify returns, a process known as leveraging. For instance, using borrowed funds to purchase real estate or stocks can yield returns that far exceed the cost of borrowing.

Risks: Potential Pitfalls

While the rewards can be substantial, debt also carries significant risks.

Interest payments on loans must be met regardless of the performance of the investment, market volatility can erode the value of leveraged assets, and overleveraging—borrowing beyond one's means—can lead to financial distress or even insolvency.

Choosing Wise Investments
Real Estate: Steady Income and Appreciation

Real estate is a popular choice for leveraging due to its potential for steady rental income and property appreciation.
Successful real estate investment requires strategic property selection and effective management. Investors must consider location, market demand, and property condition to maximize returns.

Stocks: Magnified Returns through Margin Loans

Using margin loans to invest in the stock market allows investors to purchase more shares than they could with their own capital alone, potentially magnifying returns.

However, this strategy necessitates diversification and a keen awareness of market conditions to manage the heightened risk effectively.

Business: Expansion and Market Entry

Entrepreneurs can leverage debt to expand existing businesses or enter new markets. This might involve taking out loans to invest in new equipment, hire additional staff, or develop new products. While the potential for growth is substantial, these endeavors carry inherent entrepreneurial risks that must be carefully managed.

Managing Debt Responsibly
Repayment Plan: Ensuring Manageable Obligations

A clear and realistic repayment plan is essential for managing debt responsibly. This plan should outline how debt obligations will be met without causing financial strain. Factors to consider include income, expenses, and potential changes in financial circumstances.

Emergency Fund: Financial Cushion

Maintaining an emergency fund provides a safety net for unexpected expenses or investment losses, preventing the need to take on additional debt during financial hardship. This fund should cover several months' worth of expenses to ensure financial stability.

Avoid Overleveraging: Setting Limits

Setting borrowing limits based on income and assets helps avoid overleveraging. This conservative approach protects against financial instability by ensuring that debt levels remain manageable and aligned with one's financial capacity.

Regular Review: Monitoring and Adjusting

Regularly reviewing financial goals, investment performance, and debt levels is crucial for effective debt management. Adjusting strategies based on these reviews helps maintain financial health and progress toward wealth-building objectives.

Financial Education is Key

Understanding key financial concepts is crucial for making informed decisions about leveraging debt.

Interest Rates: Fixed vs. Variable

Knowing the difference between fixed and variable interest rates—and their respective impacts on loan repayments—helps in selecting the most suitable financing options. Fixed rates offer stability, while variable rates may offer lower initial costs but carry the risk of increasing over time.

Compounding: Impact on Debt and Investments

Compounding can significantly increase the cost of debt over time, especially if interest payments are not managed effectively.

Conversely, understanding compounding can help maximize returns on investments, as reinvested earnings generate additional income.

Risk Assessment: Evaluating Investments

Assessing the risk associated with different investments is essential for strategic decision-making. This involves understanding market trends, economic conditions, and personal risk tolerance to balance potential returns with acceptable levels of risk.

Real-Life Examples

Real Estate: Jane's Story

Jane, a middle-income earner, used a mortgage to purchase rental properties. By selecting properties in high-demand areas and managing them efficiently, she generated rental income that exceeded her mortgage payments.
Over time, the properties appreciated in value, significantly increasing her net worth.

Stocks: John's Strategy

John, a tech industry professional, used margin loans to invest in high-growth tech stocks.

By diversifying his investments and staying informed about market trends, he achieved substantial returns. Although he experienced some market downturns, his overall strategy led to significant financial gains.

Business: Lisa's Expansion

Lisa, a small business owner, took out a business loan to expand her operations. She invested in new equipment and hired additional staff, increasing her production capacity and revenue. The increased profits allowed her to repay the loan quickly and continue growing her business.

Start Your Journey

Begin Small: Gain Experience

Start with manageable investments and gradually increase your exposure as you gain confidence and experience. Consider purchasing a small rental property or investing a portion of your savings in a diversified stock portfolio.

Seek Guidance: Professional Advice

Consult financial advisors for personalized advice and a sound financial plan. Advisors can offer insights into market trends, investment opportunities, and risk management, helping you navigate complex financial decisions.

Educate Yourself: Enhance Financial Literacy

Utilize online courses, books, and financial news to enhance your financial literacy. Understanding the fundamentals of finance, debt management, and investment can empower you to make informed decisions.

Technology Advantage: Efficient Management

Leverage online platforms, robo-advisors, and investment apps for efficient management of your investments. These tools offer features such as automated portfolio management, real-time market data, and educational resources.

Diversification: Mitigate Risk

Spread investments across different asset classes to mitigate risk. Diversification helps protect your portfolio from market volatility and ensures more stable returns.

Debt: A Powerful Tool, When Used Wisely Strategic debt use can be transformative. By understanding risks and rewards, choosing wise investments, and managing debt responsibly, you can leverage it for significant financial growth and stability.

"Debt to Wealth" equips you with the knowledge and tools to navigate debt and achieve financial success. Embrace this journey and thrive in today's economic landscape.

Chapter 8: Debt is Tax-Free

In the realm of personal finance and investment, understanding the nuances of how debt works can transform your approach to wealth building. One of the most compelling aspects of debt is its tax-free nature.

This chapter will explore why debt is considered tax-free, how borrowing for investment purposes can effectively provide tax-free money, and why this makes debt less expensive than equity.
We'll delve into the implications for individual investors and discuss strategies for leveraging this powerful tool to build wealth.

The Nature of Tax-Free Debt
Debt, when used strategically, can be a potent financial instrument. One of the key advantages is that the principal amount you borrow is not considered taxable income. This contrasts sharply with earned income, which is subject to various taxes.

Understanding Tax-Free Debt:

When you borrow money, the amount received does not count as income. Instead, it is a liability that must be repaid. For example, if you take out a loan of $100,000, this amount is not taxed because it is not income; it is a debt that you owe. This feature of debt makes it an attractive option for financing investments and significant purchases.

Equity vs. Debt:

Equity represents ownership in an asset, such as a business or property. When you invest equity, you are using your own money, which has already been taxed. For instance, if you earn $100,000 in salary, you might pay around $30,000 in taxes, leaving you with $70,000 to invest. This is the post-tax amount you can use for equity investments.

On the other hand, when you borrow money, you can invest the full amount of the loan. If you borrow $100,000, you have the entire sum to invest, as it is not reduced by taxes.

This makes debt a more efficient way to access capital for investments.

Interest Payments and Tax Deductions:

Interest payments on certain types of debt are tax-deductible. For example, in the United States, mortgage interest and interest on loans used for investments can be deducted from your taxable income. This deduction effectively reduces the cost of borrowing, making debt even more advantageous.

Consider an investor in a high tax bracket who borrows $100,000 at an interest rate of 5%. The annual interest payment would be $5,000. If the investor is in the 37% tax bracket, they can deduct this $5,000 from their taxable income, resulting in a tax saving of $1,850. This deduction lowers the effective interest rate, making debt a cheaper option for financing investments.

Borrowing for Investment: Tax-Free Money Borrowing to invest allows you to use debt as a tax-free source of funds.

This strategy can significantly enhance your returns and provide various financial benefits.

Real Estate Investments:

Real estate is a prime example of using debt to generate tax-free money. When you take out a mortgage to buy a property, the loan is not taxed. Moreover, the interest on the mortgage is tax-deductible, and the property can generate rental income, which can be offset by various expenses, including depreciation.

For instance, suppose you buy a rental property for $500,000 with a $400,000 mortgage. The rental income from the property is $30,000 annually.
After deducting mortgage interest, property taxes, maintenance costs, and depreciation, your taxable income from the property might be significantly reduced or even eliminated. This strategy allows you to generate cash flow while benefiting from tax deductions, making debt a highly efficient way to build wealth through real estate.

Stock Market Investments:

Margin loans are another way to use debt for investments. When you borrow money to buy stocks, the loan itself is not taxed. If you borrow $100,000 to invest in a diversified portfolio of stocks, the potential gains are based on the full amount invested, not a reduced, post-tax amount.

Moreover, if the stocks generate dividends, these can be reinvested or used to pay down the loan. The interest on the margin loan is typically tax-deductible, further reducing the cost of borrowing. By carefully selecting stocks and managing the risk, investors can leverage debt to amplify their returns and build substantial wealth.

Business Investments:

Starting or expanding a business often requires significant capital, and borrowing can be a smart way to finance these ventures. Loans used to purchase business assets or cover operational costs are not taxed as income.

Additionally, the interest on business loans is tax-deductible, reducing the effective cost of borrowing.

For example, an entrepreneur might borrow $200,000 to start a new venture. This loan can be used to purchase equipment, hire staff, and cover other startup costs.

As the business grows, the revenue generated can be used to repay the loan. Meanwhile, the interest payments reduce the business's taxable income, providing a financial cushion during the crucial early stages of growth.

Debt vs. Equity: Cost Comparison
Understanding why debt can be cheaper than equity is crucial for making informed financial decisions.

This section will compare the costs associated with debt and equity, highlighting why debt can be a more cost-effective option for financing investments.

Cost of Equity:

Equity financing involves using your own money or raising funds through investors by selling shares in your business. The cost of equity is not just the amount of money you invest but also the opportunity cost and potential taxes involved.

For example, if you earn $100,000 in salary, you might pay around $30,000 in taxes, leaving you with $70,000 to invest.

This is the cost of equity – the post-tax amount you have available. Additionally, raising equity by selling shares in your business means giving up a portion of ownership and potentially a share of future profits.

Cost of Debt:

Debt financing involves borrowing money, which is not taxed as income. The primary cost of debt is the interest you pay on the loan.

However, as previously discussed, interest payments on certain types of debt are tax-deductible, reducing the effective cost of borrowing.

Consider an investor who borrows $100,000 at an interest rate of 5%. The annual interest payment is $5,000. If the investor is in the 37% tax bracket, they can deduct this $5,000 from their taxable income, resulting in a tax saving of $1,850.
This reduces the effective interest cost to $3,150, or an effective interest rate of 3.15%. This lower effective cost makes debt a more attractive option for financing investments compared to equity, which involves post-tax money and potential loss of ownership.

Leveraging Tax Deductions:

The ability to deduct interest payments significantly lowers the cost of debt. This deduction is a powerful tool for investors, enabling them to use borrowed funds more efficiently.

By reducing taxable income, interest deductions enhance cash flow and increase the overall return on investment.

For instance, if an investor uses a loan to buy a rental property, the interest payments on the mortgage are deductible, reducing the investor's tax liability. This makes the investment more profitable and provides a cushion against market fluctuations.

Similarly, businesses can deduct interest payments on loans used for operational expenses or expansion, lowering their taxable income and freeing up cash for further investment.

Strategies for Leveraging Debt
To maximize the benefits of debt, it's essential to develop strategies that align with your financial goals and risk tolerance. This section will discuss various strategies for leveraging debt effectively.

Real Estate:

Cash Flow Analysis:

Before purchasing a rental property, conduct a thorough cash flow analysis. Ensure that the rental income will cover mortgage payments, property taxes, insurance, maintenance, and other expenses.
Positive cash flow is crucial for managing debt and generating profits.

Equity Building:

Use rental income to pay down the mortgage and build equity in the property. Over time, as the mortgage balance decreases and property values appreciate, your equity will increase, providing a substantial return on investment.
Refinancing:

Consider refinancing your mortgage to take advantage of lower interest rates. Refinancing can reduce your monthly payments, improve cash flow, and free up funds for additional investments.

Stock Market:

Margin Investing:

Use margin loans to increase your investment in stocks. Carefully select stocks with strong growth potential and diversify your portfolio to manage risk. Monitor the market closely and set stop-loss orders to protect your investments. Dividend Reinvestment:

Reinvest dividends from your stock portfolio to take advantage of compounding returns. Reinvesting dividends increases your investment's value over time and enhances your overall returns.

Long-Term Perspective:

Maintain a long-term perspective when investing with borrowed funds. Market fluctuations are inevitable, but a diversified portfolio of quality stocks will likely appreciate over time, providing substantial returns.

Business Ventures:

Strategic Borrowing:

Use loans strategically to finance business expansion, purchase equipment, or cover operational costs. Ensure that the borrowed funds will generate sufficient revenue to cover interest payments and provide a return on investment.

Cash Flow Management:

Maintain a strong focus on cash flow management. Monitor your cash flow regularly, manage expenses, and ensure you have sufficient reserves to cover debt obligations and unexpected expenses.

Growth Financing:

Leverage debt to finance growth opportunities, such as entering new markets, launching new products, or acquiring other businesses. Growth financing can significantly enhance your business's value and profitability.

Real-Life Applications and Case Studies

Understanding theoretical concepts is important, but seeing how these strategies are applied in real life can provide valuable insights.

This section will explore real-life applications and case studies, showcasing how individuals and businesses use debt to build wealth.

Personal Finance Stories of Debt Success:

Real Estate Investment:

Jane, a middle-income earner, used a mortgage to purchase rental properties. By carefully selecting properties in high-demand areas and managing them efficiently, she generated rental income that exceeded her mortgage payments. Over time, the properties appreciated in value, significantly increasing her net worth.

Stock Market Investment:

John, a tech industry professional, used margin loans to invest in high-growth tech stocks.

By diversifying his investments and staying informed about market trends, he achieved substantial returns. Although he experienced some market downturns, his overall strategy led to significant financial gains.

Small Business Expansion:

Lisa, a small business owner, took out a business loan to expand her operations. She invested in new equipment and hired additional staff, increasing her production capacity and revenue. The increased profits allowed her to repay the loan quickly and continue growing her business.

How Everyday Americans Can Implement These Strategies:

Start Small:

Begin with manageable investments and gradually increase your exposure as you gain confidence and experience.

For example, consider purchasing a small rental property or investing a portion of your savings in a diversified stock portfolio.
Seek Professional Advice:

Consulting with financial advisors or investment professionals can provide valuable guidance and help you develop a sound financial strategy. Advisors can offer insights into market trends, investment opportunities, and risk management.

Educate Yourself:

Take advantage of financial literacy resources, such as online courses, workshops, and books. Understanding the fundamentals of finance, debt management, and investment can empower you to make informed decisions.
Leverage Technology:

Use online trading platforms, robo-advisors, and investment apps to manage your investments efficiently. These tools offer features such as automated portfolio management, real-time market data, and educational resources.

Diversify Your Investments:
Spread your investments across different asset classes and industries to reduce risk. Diversification can help protect your portfolio from market volatility and ensure more stable returns.

Tools and Resources for Financial Education:

Online Courses:

Many institutions offer online courses on personal finance, investing, and debt management. Websites such as Coursera, Udemy, and Khan Academy provide valuable educational content.

Books:

Numerous books offer insights into financial strategies and debt management.
Titles such as "Rich Dad Poor Dad" by Robert Kiyosaki and "The Intelligent Investor" by Benjamin Graham provide practical advice on building wealth.

Financial News:

Staying informed about market trends and economic developments is crucial. Websites like Bloomberg, CNBC, and The Wall Street Journal offer up-to-date financial news and analysis.

Professional Advisors:

Financial advisors and planners can provide personalized advice based on your financial goals and situation. They can help you develop a comprehensive financial plan and guide you through complex investment decisions.

Investment Apps:

Apps like Robinhood, Acorns, and Betterment offer user-friendly platforms for managing investments. These apps provide features such as automated investing, portfolio tracking, and educational resources.

The strategic use of debt can be a powerful tool for building wealth, particularly for the wealthy who understand how to leverage it effectively.

By taking advantage of tax breaks, leveraging investments, and managing risks, affluent individuals and businesses can amplify their returns and accumulate wealth at a much faster rate.

Understanding how to use debt strategically requires financial education, careful planning, and informed decision-making. By embracing these principles, individuals at all income levels can leverage debt to achieve financial growth and stability.

"Debt to Wealth: Mastering Financial Leverage" aims to provide readers with the knowledge and tools to navigate the complexities of debt and leverage it for financial success. Embrace this journey, and you will be well-prepared to thrive in an ever-changing economic environment.

Chapter 9: The Dollar Becomes Debt

In the modern financial system, debt and currency are deeply intertwined. The U.S. dollar, in particular, has become synonymous with debt due to the way it is created and circulated within the economy.

This chapter will explore the connection between debt and the money supply, how government spending is financed through debt, and the broader economic implications for citizens. Understanding these concepts is crucial for comprehending the dynamics of the current financial landscape and making informed decisions.

The Connection Between Debt and Money Supply

To understand how the dollar has become debt, it is essential to grasp the relationship between debt and money creation.

In today's economy, money is primarily created through lending activities, both by commercial banks and through government borrowing.

Money Creation Through Lending:

When a commercial bank issues a loan, it essentially creates new money. This process starts when a borrower takes out a loan, and the bank credits the borrower's account with the loan amount.
This transaction increases the money supply because the borrower now has more money to spend, while the bank records the loan as an asset.

For example, if you take out a $100,000 mortgage to buy a house, the bank credits your account with $100,000. This money did not exist in the physical form before the loan was issued; it was created through the act of lending.
The borrower now has $100,000 to spend, which increases the money supply in the economy.

Government Borrowing and Money Supply:

The government also plays a significant role in money creation through borrowing. When the U.S. Treasury issues bonds to finance government spending, these bonds are often purchased by the Federal Reserve or commercial banks.

The purchase of these bonds injects money into the economy, thereby increasing the money supply.

For instance, if the government issues $1 billion in bonds and the Federal Reserve buys these bonds, the Fed credits the government's account with $1 billion.
This money can then be spent on various government programs, increasing the money supply.

The bonds held by the Fed represent government debt, which must be repaid with interest in the future.

Quantitative Easing (QE):

Quantitative easing is a monetary policy tool used by central banks to increase the money supply by purchasing government bonds and other financial assets. This process involves creating new money to buy these assets, which injects liquidity into the economy.

During the global financial crisis of 2008 and the COVID-19 pandemic, the Federal Reserve implemented QE to stabilize the economy.

By purchasing large quantities of government bonds, the Fed increased the money supply, lowered interest rates, and encouraged borrowing and spending.

While QE helped to prevent economic collapse, it also significantly increased the amount of money in circulation and contributed to the rise in government debt.

Financing Government Spending Through Debt

Government spending is often financed through borrowing,
allowing the government to fund essential programs and services without immediately raising taxes.
This approach has both benefits and drawbacks, impacting the economy and citizens in various ways.

Budget Deficits and Borrowing:

A budget deficit occurs when government expenditures exceed revenues. To finance this deficit, the government issues bonds to raise capital from investors. These bonds are essentially IOUs, promising to pay back the principal amount along with interest at a future date.

For example, during economic recessions, tax revenues typically decline as businesses earn less and unemployment rises. Simultaneously, government spending on social programs, such as unemployment benefits and healthcare, increases.

This combination of lower revenues and higher expenditures results in budget deficits, necessitating borrowing to cover the shortfall.

Long-Term Investments and Economic Growth:

Borrowing allows the government to make long-term investments in infrastructure, education, healthcare, and other critical areas. These investments can stimulate economic growth, improve public services, and enhance the quality of life for citizens.

For instance, borrowing to build highways, bridges, and public transportation systems creates jobs, reduces transportation costs, and boosts economic productivity.
Investing in education improves the skills and productivity of the workforce, leading to higher economic growth and increased tax revenues in the future.

Counter-Cyclical Fiscal Policy:
Government borrowing also enables the implementation of counter-cyclical fiscal policies.

During economic downturns, the government can increase spending and borrowing to stimulate the economy,
while during periods of growth, it can reduce spending and pay down debt.

For example, during the COVID-19 pandemic, the U.S. government implemented massive stimulus packages to support individuals and businesses. These measures included direct payments to citizens, enhanced unemployment benefits, and loans to small businesses.

While these measures increased government debt, they helped prevent a deeper economic recession by maintaining consumer spending and business operations.

The Economic Implications for Citizens
The relationship between debt and currency has significant implications for citizens.
Understanding these implications can help individuals make informed financial decisions and advocate for responsible fiscal policies.

Interest Payments and Fiscal Burden:

One of the primary concerns with high levels of government debt is the burden of interest payments. As the debt grows, so do the interest payments, which must be financed through taxes or additional borrowing. High interest payments can limit the government's ability to fund essential services and investments, potentially leading to higher taxes or reduced public spending.

For example, in 2022, the U.S. government spent approximately $400 billion on interest payments for its debt. This amount is expected to rise as the debt increases and interest rates potentially go up. Higher interest payments mean fewer resources are available for other critical areas, such as healthcare, education, and infrastructure.

Inflation and Purchasing Power:

Excessive government borrowing can lead to inflation if it results in an excessive increase in the money supply.

Inflation erodes the purchasing power of money, making goods and services more expensive for consumers.
This can have a disproportionate impact on low- and middle-income households, who may struggle to keep up with rising costs.

Inflation also affects interest rates, as central banks may raise rates to control inflation. Higher interest rates can increase borrowing costs for individuals and businesses, potentially slowing economic growth.

Taxation and Public Services:

To manage high levels of debt, governments may need to increase taxes or cut public spending. Higher taxes reduce disposable income for individuals and businesses, potentially slowing economic growth. Cuts to public services can impact the quality of education, healthcare, and infrastructure, affecting the overall well-being of citizens.

For example, austerity measures implemented in some countries to manage debt levels have led to significant reductions in public services and social programs, adversely affecting vulnerable populations.

Economic Stability and Investor Confidence:

Responsible debt management is essential for maintaining economic stability and investor confidence. High levels of debt can undermine confidence in a country's ability to repay its obligations, potentially leading to higher borrowing costs and financial instability.

Investors consider a country's debt levels when deciding where to invest. High debt levels can signal financial instability and increase the perceived risk of investing in that country. Conversely, responsible debt management can enhance investor confidence, attract foreign investment, and support economic growth.

The Future of Debt and Currency

The relationship between debt and currency is likely to continue evolving in response to economic conditions, policy decisions, and technological advancements. Understanding these dynamics is crucial for navigating the complexities of the modern financial system.

Technological Innovations:

Technological advancements, such as digital currencies and blockchain technology, have the potential to transform the financial system.

Central banks worldwide are exploring the development of central bank digital currencies (CBDCs) to enhance payment systems and improve monetary policy effectiveness.

Digital currencies could change the way money is created and circulated, potentially reducing reliance on traditional banking systems and altering the dynamics of debt and money supply.

However, the widespread adoption of digital currencies also poses challenges, such as cybersecurity risks and regulatory considerations.

Fiscal and Monetary Policy Coordination:

Effective coordination between fiscal and monetary policy will remain essential for managing debt and economic stability. Governments and central banks must work together to balance the need for economic stimulus with the risks of inflation and financial instability.

For instance, during economic crises, coordinated efforts between fiscal stimulus measures and monetary policy actions, such as QE, can provide a more comprehensive approach to stabilizing the economy. Conversely, during periods of economic growth, coordinated efforts to reduce deficits and manage debt levels can help ensure long-term sustainability.

Global Economic Shifts:

Global economic shifts, such as changes in trade dynamics, demographic trends, and geopolitical developments, will also influence the relationship between debt and currency. For example, an aging population in many developed countries may increase demand for social services and healthcare, leading to higher government spending and debt.

Geopolitical developments, such as trade tensions and changes in international alliances, can impact global capital flows and demand for reserve currencies. Understanding these shifts and their implications for debt and currency is crucial for navigating the future financial landscape.

The intricate relationship between debt and money supply is a cornerstone of the modern financial system. Understanding how debt functions as money, the role of government borrowing in financing public expenditures, and the economic implications for citizens is crucial for making informed financial decisions.

Government borrowing allows for critical investments and economic stabilization, but it also carries significant responsibilities and risks. Managing debt levels and ensuring fiscal responsibility are essential for maintaining economic stability and supporting long-term growth.

As the global financial system continues to evolve, staying informed about the dynamics of debt and currency will be increasingly important. By leveraging the principles of debt management and investment, individuals can navigate the complexities of the financial landscape and achieve lasting financial success.

"Debt to Wealth: Mastering Financial Leverage" aims to equip readers with the knowledge and tools to understand and harness the power of debt for financial growth. Embrace this journey, and you will be well-prepared to thrive in an ever-changing economic environment.

Chapter 10: The Benefits of Debt for the Wealthy

 In contemporary finance, debt is often seen as a tool to be avoided, particularly by those who struggle to manage their finances. However, for the wealthy, debt can be a powerful instrument for wealth creation and financial leverage.

This chapter explores how affluent individuals and businesses use debt to their advantage, leveraging investments for significant returns, and examines the growing wealth gap and its implications.

Tax Breaks and Interest Payments
One of the significant advantages of debt for the wealthy is the tax benefits associated with interest payments. In many tax systems, interest paid on loans for investment purposes can be deducted from taxable income, reducing the overall tax burden.

Mortgage Interest Deduction:
In the United States, for instance, homeowners can deduct the interest paid on their mortgage from their taxable income. This deduction can be substantial, especially for high-income individuals with large mortgages. By reducing taxable income, the mortgage interest deduction effectively lowers the cost of borrowing.

The impact of this deduction can be illustrated with a simple example. Suppose a high-income individual purchases a luxury home with a mortgage of $2 million at an interest rate of 3.5%. The annual interest payment would be $70,000.

If this individual is in the 37% federal tax bracket, the mortgage interest deduction would reduce their taxable income by $70,000, resulting in a tax saving of $25,900. This effectively lowers the cost of the mortgage, making it a financially savvy move for those who can afford it.

Investment Loan Interest:
Interest on loans used to purchase investments, such as stocks or real estate, can also be deductible. This means that wealthy individuals can borrow money to invest and then deduct the interest payments on those loans from their taxable income. This strategy not only reduces the cost of borrowing but also enhances the net returns on investments.

For example, if an investor takes out a $1 million loan at an interest rate of 4% to purchase real estate and earns an 8% return on the investment, they can deduct the $40,000 in annual interest payments from their taxable income. If they are in a high tax bracket, this deduction can significantly reduce their overall tax liability. This ability to deduct interest payments effectively lowers the cost of leveraging investments, making it a powerful tool for building wealth.

Leveraging Investments for Significant Returns
The wealthy often use debt to leverage their investments, amplifying potential returns.

This strategy involves borrowing money at a lower interest rate to invest in assets that are expected to generate higher returns. While leveraging can increase both gains and losses, it is a common tactic among affluent investors who can manage the associated risks.

Real Estate Investments:
Real estate is a popular asset class for leveraging. Wealthy individuals and businesses often use mortgages to finance property purchases, allowing them to control valuable assets with relatively little of their own capital. Rental income and property appreciation can generate substantial returns, often exceeding the cost of borrowing.

Consider a real estate investor who purchases a $5 million commercial property with a $1 million down payment and a $4 million mortgage at an interest rate of 3.5%. If the property generates $400,000 in annual rental income and appreciates by 5% per year, the investor's return on equity can be significantly higher than if they had purchased the property outright.

The rental income covers the mortgage payments, and the appreciation increases the property's value, enhancing the investor's overall return.

In addition to rental income and appreciation, real estate investments offer other financial benefits, such as depreciation deductions.

Depreciation allows investors to deduct a portion of the property's value from their taxable income each year, further reducing their tax liability. These combined benefits make real estate a powerful tool for wealth creation when leveraged effectively.

Stock Market Investments:
Margin loans are another way the wealthy leverage investments. By borrowing money to purchase stocks, investors can increase their exposure to the market and potentially achieve higher returns. However, margin investing also carries higher risk, as losses can be magnified in a market downturn.

Consider an investor with a $1 million portfolio who borrows an additional $500,000 at an interest rate of 5% to purchase more stocks. If the stock portfolio appreciates by 10%, the investor earns $150,000 on their $1.5 million investment. After paying $25,000 in interest, the net gain is $125,000, representing a 12.5% return on the initial $1 million, compared to a 10% return without leverage.

While the potential for higher returns is attractive, margin investing requires careful risk management.
Market volatility can lead to significant losses, especially if the value of the stocks falls below the loan amount. Wealthy investors often mitigate this risk by diversifying their portfolios and using stop-loss orders to limit potential losses.

Private Equity and Venture Capital:
Wealthy individuals often invest in private equity and venture capital, which involve providing capital to private companies in exchange for equity ownership.

These investments can offer high returns, particularly if the companies experience significant growth or are acquired. Leveraging debt to finance these investments can enhance returns, although the risks are also higher compared to traditional investments.

Private equity investments typically involve purchasing a significant stake in a company and working to improve its operations and profitability. This hands-on approach can lead to substantial returns when the company is eventually sold or goes public. Venture capital, on the other hand, involves investing in early-stage companies with high growth potential. While the risks are greater, successful venture capital investments can yield returns many times the initial investment.

For example, consider a venture capitalist who invests $1 million in a startup with high growth potential. To finance the investment, they take out a $500,000 loan at an interest rate of 6%. If the startup grows rapidly and is acquired for $10 million, the venture capitalist's equity stake could be worth $5 million.

After repaying the loan and interest, the net return on the initial investment is significantly enhanced.

The Growing Wealth Gap and Its Implications
The strategic use of debt by the wealthy contributes to the growing wealth gap. As affluent individuals and businesses leverage debt to enhance their returns, they can accumulate wealth at a much faster rate than those who rely solely on their own capital or traditional savings methods.

Income and Wealth Disparity:
Income and wealth disparity have been increasing globally, with a significant portion of wealth concentrated among the top 1% of earners. The ability to use debt effectively is a key factor in this disparity. While middle- and lower-income individuals often use debt for consumption, such as credit card debt or auto loans, the wealthy use debt to invest in appreciating assets.

This disparity is evident in the types of debt held by different income groups.

According to data from the Federal Reserve, higher-income households are more likely to hold mortgage debt and investment loans, while lower-income households are more likely to carry credit card debt and personal loans. The former types of debt are used to acquire assets that can appreciate and generate income, while the latter often finance consumption and do not contribute to wealth building.

Economic Mobility:
The growing wealth gap has implications for economic mobility. Those with access to capital and financial knowledge can leverage debt to create more wealth, while those without such access may struggle to build financial security. This disparity can lead to reduced social and economic mobility, where the wealthy have more opportunities to invest in education, business ventures, and other wealth-building activities.

For example, access to education is a significant factor in economic mobility.

Wealthy families can afford to send their children to prestigious schools and universities, providing them with valuable skills and networks. In contrast, lower-income families may struggle to afford higher education, limiting their children's opportunities for upward mobility.

Policy Considerations:
Addressing the wealth gap requires thoughtful policy interventions. Policies that promote financial education, access to credit for small businesses, and affordable housing can help bridge the gap.

Additionally, tax policies that encourage investment in underserved communities and provide incentives for wealth-building activities among lower- and middle-income individuals can promote more equitable economic growth.

For instance, policies that support affordable housing initiatives can help lower-income families build equity through homeownership.

Programs that provide grants or low-interest loans to small businesses can enable entrepreneurs to start or expand their businesses, creating jobs and stimulating economic growth.

Financial education programs can empower individuals to make informed decisions about debt and investment, helping them build wealth over time.

Social Implications:
The growing wealth gap also has social implications. Economic inequality can lead to social unrest, decreased trust in institutions, and increased political polarization.

Addressing these issues requires a comprehensive approach that includes economic, educational, and social policies aimed at creating a more inclusive and equitable society.

For example, economic inequality can lead to social tensions as those who feel left behind become frustrated with the lack of opportunities.

This frustration can manifest in various forms, including protests and political movements advocating for change. Building a more inclusive society requires addressing the root causes of inequality and creating pathways for economic mobility for all individuals.

Learning to Use Debt Strategically
For many, learning to use debt effectively can be a game-changer. This involves understanding the risks and rewards of borrowing, choosing investments wisely, and managing debt responsibly.

Financial education plays a crucial role in this process, empowering individuals to leverage debt for wealth creation rather than falling into the trap of high-interest consumer debt.

Financial Education:
Education is the foundation for effective debt management. Understanding concepts such as interest rates, compounding, and risk assessment is crucial for making informed decisions.

Financial literacy programs can provide individuals with the knowledge and skills needed to manage debt and investments effectively.

For example, financial education can help individuals understand the difference between good debt and bad debt. Good debt, such as a mortgage or student loan, is used to acquire assets that can appreciate and generate income.
Bad debt, such as credit card debt or high-interest personal loans, is often used for consumption and does not contribute to wealth building.

Investment Strategies:
Choosing the right investments is key to leveraging debt successfully.

Real estate, stocks, and business ventures can all provide substantial returns, but they also carry varying levels of risk. Diversifying investments can help manage risk and ensure more stable returns.

Risk Management:
Effective debt management involves understanding and mitigating risks.
This includes having a clear repayment plan, maintaining an emergency fund, and avoiding overleveraging.
By managing risks, individuals can use debt to enhance their financial growth without exposing themselves to undue financial strain.

Building Wealth Through Debt:
Building wealth through debt requires a strategic approach.

This involves setting clear financial goals, creating a budget, and consistently investing in assets that appreciate over time. Regularly reviewing and adjusting financial plans ensures that debt is used effectively to achieve financial objectives.

Real-Life Applications of Debt Strategies
Understanding theoretical concepts is important, but seeing how these strategies are applied in real life can provide valuable insights. This section will explore real-life applications of debt strategies, showcasing how individuals and businesses use debt to build wealth.

Personal Finance Stories of Debt Success:

Real Estate Investment:
Jane, a middle-income earner, used a mortgage to purchase rental properties. By carefully selecting properties in high-demand areas and managing them efficiently, she generated rental income that exceeded her mortgage payments. Over time, the properties appreciated in value, significantly increasing her net worth.

Stock Market Investment:
John, a tech industry professional, used margin loans to invest in high-growth tech stocks. By diversifying his investments and staying informed about market trends, he achieved substantial returns.

Although he experienced some market downturns, his overall strategy led to significant financial gains.

Small Business Expansion:
Lisa, a small business owner, took out a business loan to expand her operations. She invested in new equipment and hired additional staff, increasing her production capacity and revenue. The increased profits allowed her to repay the loan quickly and continue growing her business.

How Everyday Americans Can Implement These Strategies:

Start Small:
Begin with manageable investments and gradually increase your exposure as you gain confidence and experience. For example, consider purchasing a small rental property or investing a portion of your savings in a diversified stock portfolio.

Seek Professional Advice:
Consulting with financial advisors or investment professionals can provide valuable guidance and help you develop a sound financial strategy. Advisors can offer insights into market trends, investment opportunities, and risk management.

Educate Yourself:
Take advantage of financial literacy resources, such as online courses, workshops, and books. Understanding the fundamentals of finance, debt management, and investment can empower you to make informed decisions.

Leverage Technology:
Use online trading platforms, robo-advisors, and investment apps to manage your investments efficiently. These tools offer features such as automated portfolio management, real-time market data, and educational resources.

Diversify Your Investments:
Spread your investments across different asset classes and industries to reduce risk.

Diversification can help protect your portfolio from market volatility and ensure more stable returns.

Tools and Resources for Financial Education:

Online Courses:
Many institutions offer online courses on personal finance, investing, and debt management. Websites such as Coursera, Udemy, and Khan Academy provide valuable educational content.

Books:
Numerous books offer insights into financial strategies and debt management. Titles such as "Rich Dad Poor Dad" by Robert Kiyosaki and "The Intelligent Investor" by Benjamin Graham provide practical advice on building wealth.

Financial News:
Staying informed about market trends and economic developments is crucial. Websites like Bloomberg, CNBC, and The Wall Street Journal offer up-to-date financial news and analysis.

Professional Advisors:
Financial advisors and planners can provide personalized advice based on your financial goals and situation. They can help you develop a comprehensive financial plan and guide you through complex investment decisions.

Investment Apps:
Apps like Robinhood, Acorns, and Betterment offer user-friendly platforms for managing investments. These apps provide features such as automated investing, portfolio tracking, and educational resources.

The strategic use of debt can be a powerful tool for building wealth, particularly for the wealthy who understand how to leverage it effectively. By taking advantage of tax breaks, leveraging investments, and managing risks, affluent individuals and businesses can amplify their returns and accumulate wealth at a much faster rate.

Understanding how to use debt strategically requires financial education, careful planning, and informed decision-making.

By embracing these principles, individuals at all income levels can leverage debt to achieve financial growth and stability.

"Debt to Wealth: Mastering Financial Leverage" aims to provide readers with the knowledge and tools to navigate the complexities of debt and leverage it for financial success. Embrace this journey, and you will be well-prepared to thrive in an ever-changing economic environment.

Made in United States
Orlando, FL
26 March 2025

59862460R00095